The Roaring Twenties

A Captivating Guide to a Period of Dramatic Social and Political Change, a False Sense of Prosperity, and Its Impact on the Great Depression

Free Bonus from Captivating History (Available for a Limited time)

Hi History Lovers!

Now you have a chance to join our exclusive history list so you can get your first history ebook for free as well as discounts and a potential to get more history books for free! Simply visit the link below to join.

Captivatinghistory.com/ebook

Also, make sure to follow us on:

Twitter: @Captivhistory

Facebook: Captivating History:@captivatinghistory

Contents

Introduction

Few decades capture the imagination like the 1920s. Like so many good stories, it got its start from a time of great turmoil and ended in a dramatic fashion. What happened between 1920 and 1929 has passed beyond history and has become legend.

The event that made the 1920s was the great conflict in the previous decade, World War I. American military involvement was only for a year. However from the beginning of the war in 1914, American eyes were on Europe.

The mass destruction from the fighting, the changes wrought by the shift in the American economy, and the very flawed peace that followed the war all made a profound impact on the decade that followed. Soldiers came back from the war sometimes disturbed, sometimes broken, and almost always disillusioned. The nation experienced a great movement of people, from country to city causing changes in the makeup of cities that would not be recognizable to residents from an earlier era.

As the president looked for a "return to normalcy," the cultural and social landscape did not make any such return journey. Social causes of the early twentieth century were either disregarded or completely rejected. Other social movements took over and revealed a more conservative and isolationist country than the one that had gone to war in 1917.

The effect of the war and the decade on American literature was profound. A modern form of music, uniquely American which some consider the only true American art form, became the soundtrack of the decade. Two new forms of entertainment also altered the decade as well; motion pictures and radio moved from fringe innovations to common entertainments. Some older entertainments, especially baseball, embraced the change of the new decade. After a crippling scandal had rocked the sport in 1919, a new player, Babe Ruth, inspired a new style of baseball which made him a national phenomenon.

Like Babe Ruth and his towering home runs, the economy of the 1920s boomed and people had more money to spend, they brought more into their homes than just radios. The availability of home appliances, coupled with more money and more credit, led people to buy more. The one item that radically changed the United States, however, was the automobile.

Henry Ford took what had been an extravagance for the rich and made it affordable to the masses. With the advent of the Model T, Americans moved further and faster than ever before. In addition, the entire auto industry created or sustained industries that had been small or non-existent before. By the end of the decade, millions of Americans were in cars.

But all was not as it appeared. Certain important segments of the economy, thus the population, were being left behind. Though the boom in manufacturing brought on by the automobile and consumer goods helped many Americans, the decade saw a dramatic decline in farming. As more people than ever before embraced buying on credit, this included speculating on stocks with credit as well. This, along with other causes woven into the fabric of the decade, led to the eventual crash that closed the 1920s.

The lessons of the 1920s are still relevant today. Many of the debates and issues of the era are still part of the national conversation. Economic policies, consumer behaviors and mass culture of the

1920s are reflected in our culture almost 100 years later. By understanding the past, we can better prepare for the future.

Chapter 1 – World War One and the 1920s

In the spring of 1914, Europe was rocked by the assassination of Archduke Ferdinand and his wife in Sarajevo. The Serbian nationalist group, The Black Hand, was responsible for the murder and the Austro-Hungarian Empire demanded justice, not only by punishing the guilty party, but by sending a message to other Serbs and other subjugated people.

This was not easy to carry out. A series of agreements and alliances stretching across the continent made retaliation against the Serbs a dangerous proposition. Russia considered itself the protector of all Slavic people and pledged to defend Serbia. In turn, Germany held a strong alliance with its Germanic neighbor, Austro-Hungary, and pledged to aid them by attacking Russia. By pledging to stand against Russia, an alliance created in 1907 between France, Great Britain, and Russia was activated. Any German action against Russia was an act of war toward the other two powers. By the end of August 1914, World War I had begun.

Within the first six months of the war, the carnage on both the eastern and western fronts was unfathomable. Millions were dead, and after initial progress by the Germans, they were stopped and a stalemate ensued. Some Americans at this time could remember the high casualty counts of Civil War battles, but the news from Europe was even more shocking. New weapons, such as machine guns and chemical warfare, for example mustard gas, made the modern warfare exceptionally devastating.

Seeing this news, Americans wanted no part of the latest European conflict. The president at the time, Woodrow Wilson, made the phrase "He kept us out of the war" a key part of his reelection campaign in 1916. However, events and circumstances made that a hard campaign promise to keep.

The United States tried to remain neutral in the conflict; it was apparent that a Europe controlled by Germany would be less than ideal for American commerce. As the war continued, Germany made two fateful decisions forcing the United States hand. First was the attack on a civilian cruise ship, the Lusitania, in 1915. The cruise liner left New York bound for Great Britain. A German submarine, U-20, fired torpedoes and sank the ship off the coast of Ireland. 1,198 lost their lives, including 128 Americans. The attack was quickly condemned by the United States and much of the international community. The British government insisted that the ship was not carrying any war materiel or munitions. It was largely perceived as an act of naked aggression toward civilians. Many within and outside the US government wanted retribution for such an attack on non-combatants.

The second major condition that moved the United States toward war was a decision by the Germans. In 1917, in order to put a stranglehold on Great Britain, Germany declared open warfare on any nation shipping goods to the British Isles. This included the United States.

The final act that tilted the United States toward a declaration of war on Germany was an intercepted telegram from Germany to Mexico. Referred to as the Zimmerman Telegram, the German government made overtures to Mexico, encouraging Mexico to attack the United States. All that Mexico needed to do was occupy the United States long enough for Germany to defeat Great Britain and France. After the war was over, Germany would help the Mexicans defeat the United States and help restore the US-Mexican border of the 1840s, before the Mexican-American War.

When the Zimmerman Telegram was made public, opinion shifted greatly toward entering the war on the side of the Allies. On April 2, 1917, President Woodrow Wilson asked Congress for an official declaration of war on the German Empire. The Senate voted 82-6 in favor of war and the House of Representatives voted 373-50 in favor.

With the declaration of war, American society and culture changed dramatically. All segments of the nation were geared toward the war effort. Large sections of the economy were controlled by the government as well as consumer activity. The War Industries Board made certain that American manufacturers were doing their part to ensure American victory overseas. This meant changes in production, from consumer goods to military ones. It also meant making sure that factories were running at full capacity.

It also meant a limit on the amount of goods and the availability of goods to consumers. Foodstuffs were especially important to the war effort. Citizens were encouraged to forgo meat and wheat in order to help feed the troops. The victory garden, homegrown vegetables, became a staple of American homes during the war. Herbert Hoover, the head of the Food Administration, was proud of his administration's efforts that led to a fifteen percent reduction in consumption.

One of the commodities that was of particular interest was alcohol. Grain was considered vital to the war effort; therefore, the consumption of alcoholic beverages was greatly curtailed through prohibitionary laws. Part of the push toward the prohibition of alcohol had little to do with war production or supply, but as a means to achieve a long-standing goal of progressive politicians and reformers. In addition to the argument regarding the importance of alcohol to the war effort, groups such as the Anti-Saloon League and Women's Christian Temperance Union stressed the benefits of a sober workforce and army. The success of wartime prohibition paved the way toward a more permanent ban on alcohol at the end of the decade.

In addition to regulating alcohol production and consumption, the federal government formed other agencies directing public life. The Committee on Public Information (CPI) was founded in 1917. This organization was designed for publicity; some would say propaganda. The famed Uncle Sam poster (I Want You!) originates from this period. The office also made the message of the war about a fight for the very soul of civilization, calling the enemy Huns instead of Germans and highlighting that this foreign nation was ruled by a Kaiser, not democracy.

The CPI was also responsible for providing the press with updates about the war overseas and the work of the Wilson Administration. Its goal was to inundate journalists with press releases promoting messages that the government wanted, to control the narrative to use a modern phrase. Many see the efforts of the CPI as the dawning of modern public relations.

The efforts of the CPI perhaps worked too well in some instances. One of the oldest and most established immigrant groups to the United States, German-Americans, were confronted with discrimination that they had rarely encountered since they began arriving in the United States before the Revolutionary War. Other immigrant groups, most notably the Irish, had faced a great deal of resistance from native-born Americans, but the Germans had an easier path of assimilation. That all changed with World War One. German-Americans faced a great deal of harassment in their communities, including threats of violence. The replica statue of Rodin's The Thinker in Chicago needed to be moved indoors because of vandalism.

Also, in Chicago for example, thousands of German-Americans changed their surnames because of the anti-German sentiment throughout the city. More broadly, anti-German sentiment was expressed by changing names of common food items. Sauerkraut was now called liberty cabbage, frankfurters were hot dogs, and hamburgers were referred to as Salisbury steaks. The most disturbing act of anti-German sentiment was the lynching of a

German-American man in Collinsville, Illinois because the townspeople were convinced he was a spy for Germany. All who were tried for his murder were acquitted.

Besides citizens willfully changing the names of German-American food items, the US government curtailed free speech with the passage of the Espionage Act of 1917. This made it illegal for anyone to interfere with the war efforts of the United States government. A number of cases were tried under the law and found the defendants guilty of violating the act. Two of the most notable were the convictions of Eugene Debs, a prominent socialist and union organizer, who was found guilty under the Sedition Act an amendment of the Espionage Act. The other was Charles Schenck, another socialist speaking out against the draft and the war in general. Debs was imprisoned for five years after giving a speech denouncing the war, and the case against Schenck established some of the most well-known limits of the First Amendment.

Both ideas written by Supreme Court Justice Oliver Wendell Holmes likened Schenck's anti-war mailings to imminent dangers, or to use Holmes's phrase, "clear and present danger." In addition, Holmes classified speaking out against the draft as the same misuse of free speech as yelling fire in a crowded room. As the war ended, the mechanisms set up by the court decisions and the wide latitude given to the government through the Espionage Act allowed for the prosecution (and deportation) of other critics of the United States government. Even as the Espionage Act became less relevant, the anti-socialist and anti-communist feelings that it encouraged appeared immediately after the war and into the 1920s.

As industry hummed and reached peak production, the need for workers became more and more crucial. Even before the US entry into the war, labor scarcity was becoming a problem for American manufacturers. When the draft was instituted for the war effort, the situation became dire. In order to meet the demand of industry, a relatively untapped source of labor was recruited and accepted by American companies, African-Americans from the southern states.

After the Civil War and the emancipation of the slaves in the South, there was a brief period of mobility for African-Americans, largely across the South as many former slaves searched for family members. However, as the period of Reconstruction ended in 1877, the ability of African-Americans to move freely was greatly curtailed, by customs, local laws, and intimidation. Further, the post-war economy offered little to the newly freed slaves, so the greatest opportunity for employment for African-Americans was sharecropping on the large plantations. Many former slaves even worked on the same plantations on which they were slaves.

This system remained intact into the twentieth century. It was even bolstered as southern state governments restructured their governments to severely curtail African-American voting rights. Even the federal courts reaffirmed this racial hierarchy with various decisions, most importantly Plessy v. Ferguson, which established the doctrine of separate but equal.

Events in between 1915-1917 led to a dramatic change in the demographics of the United States and the fortunes of African-Americans. Two events were based in the South and focused on the agrarian economy of the region. First, poor weather made for poor cotton harvests in both 1911 and 1912. Second, and especially detrimental to the cotton crop, was the infestation of the boll weevil. This insect wreaked havoc on southern agriculture, severely hurting sharecroppers. Such poor conditions made it a necessity for African-Americans to look for alternatives.

The event that led to those more lucrative alternatives was World War One. As factories continued to need more and more workers, African-Americans moved north to fill the employment void. In the period from 1914 to 1920, close to one third of all African-Americans moved from the rural world of the South to the urban centers of the North. The African-American population of cities like Chicago, New York, and Pittsburgh exploded, seemingly overnight. Later remembered as the Great Migration, it was one of the largest movements of people across the United States ever.

This was time of cultural exchange, upheaval, and tension. Small African-American communities in northern cities became much larger, and African-Americans who were already settled in the North were wary of their new neighbors and their country ways. Whites living in cities were fearful of the growing number of African-Americans and were determined to keep African-Americans in specific neighborhoods throughout their cities. These neighborhoods would become epicenters of culture in the next decade.

Whites in the North weren't the only people trying to keep African-Americans in their societally assigned place. Throughout the South, white newspapers published articles detailing how African-Americans could not tolerate the cold winters of the North. The newspapers also highlighted any story that showed the racial prejudice of the northern communities. Many southern communities refused to let African-Americans buy tickets for out-of-state destinations or kept them bound to their sharecropping contracts. If all else failed, threatening violence on those that tried to leave was employed. It was all to no avail. Hundreds of thousands of African-Americans made the move north in hopes of a better life with no intention of returning.

Those that went to war, some 4.7 million American men, 320,000 never returned, had as profound an experience as those on the home front. Like the young European men three years earlier, the young Americans going off to war had visions of a grand adventure and fighting for home and valor, like the Civil War heroes that many of these men knew as grandparents and other older relatives. Also like those Europeans, the Americans were quickly disillusioned about the glory of war. By the time the Americans arrived under the command of John J. Pershing, the Europeans had been fighting in the trenches and doing whatever they could to survive. The fresh-faced "doughboys" were a curiosity more than anything else.

Even if the American soldiers were green, they provided something to the Allies the German Army could not get—fresh bodies. The relationship between the American leadership and that of the French and British was often tense, especially with the Americans refusing the Allied commanders to command any of their troops. Though this would change a bit in the spring of 1918, overall the American troops retained their independence.

The fighting style of the Americans was also novel to the Europeans. As often as they could, the American commanders preferred to engage in strategic mobile warfare. The idea was to get out of the trenches and take the fight to the Germans whenever possible. The energy of the Americans proved pivotal to bringing about the armistice of November 1918. The Americans did not necessarily win the war, but they certainly caused it to end much sooner than it would have otherwise. The fight for survival, however, wasn't over once the bullets stopped flying.

Unfortunately, for many American soldiers, it wasn't the battlefront that killed them, but disease, specifically the Influenza Pandemic of 1918-1919. Estimates vary between 20 to 50 million people worldwide died because of the disease. No area of the globe was spared from the outbreak. The first wave of the epidemic started in January of 1918, but the flu mutated and became far deadlier by the fall of that year, and the death rate soared before finally reducing in the spring of 1919. It is still one of the worst medical disasters to ever occur in the world.

As the troops mustered out and returned home, they were returning as different men. The shared experiences of the soldiers would give so many of the generation a common memory, providing a backdrop for the ensuing decade. The peace process finished in 1919, the world and even the United States didn't quite realize how powerful they had truly become. At the end of the Second World War it was apparent, but at the end of the First World War, America was like a young adult finally realizing that they were stronger and nimbler than their parents. The United States, with all of those that had experienced the war in some fashion, realized over the course of the next decade exactly how far they had progressed.

Chapter 2 – Fear of the Other

Four months after the first US troops arrived in France, an event occurred that had great repercussions for the United States and the world. In October of 1917 (November 1917 Julian Calendar) the Bolsheviks in Russia overthrew the government and declared a new regime. It was a government dedicated to the writings of Karl Marx and Fredrick Engels— in short, communism. Vladimir Lenin and Leon Trotsky along with others established the Politburo and were seen immediately as a threat to most of Western Europe and the United States. Their withdrawal from World War One did little to allay those fears. In 1918, an allied force including US troops landed in Russia with hopes of stopping the spread of the Bolshevik Revolution. It was the first military intervention by the United States to stop the spread of communism.

Closer to home, after the war in 1919, strikes and unrest spread throughout the United States. Massive strikes from Seattle (a general strike) to Boston (police strike) to the steel industry made many fear that a communist revolution was coming to the United States. Further stoking that fear was the eruption of race riots across the country, the largest and most deadly occurring in Chicago. Many believed that outside agitators had a hand in starting the unrest.

After a series of mail bombings, public opinion insisted on some kind of action. The Department of Justice conducted a series of raids on known socialists, communists, and anarchists. Remembered as the Palmer Raids, named after Attorney General Mitchell Palmer, these actions took extralegal measures to round up their targets. Some of those arrested were deported. On January 2, 1920, the very beginning of the new decade, the fears of the prevailing decade were still dictating government action. A massive arrest in over 30 cities rounded up thousands of people suspected of being communists. The next day, even more arrests were made. Such a large action was met with suspicion about its legality. Communism was still seen as a threat, but after it was revealed that the Palmer Raids used unconstitutional and sometimes brutal measures to arrest their subjects, public support of such actions declined.

The Palmer Raids and the failed strikes of 1919 stymied the labor movement in the United States throughout the 1920s. Union membership dropped to its lowest level since the turn of the twentieth century. In addition, the craft unions that were the strength of the labor movement did not have a place in the growing industrial workplace. The large corporations that dominated manufacturing in the 1920s experienced a great deal of growth throughout most of the decade and were able to pay and treat their employees better than in previous generations.

The greatest purveyor of this kinder and gentler workplace was Henry Ford and his automobile manufacturing plants. Inspired by the "disassembly" line of the Chicago Stockyards, Ford perfected the assembly line for the production of the Model T, the automotive symbol of the 1920s. Ford paid his workers better than any of his competitors, gave them better hours, and even gave the entire plant Sunday off. Most memorably, Ford allowed his workers to buy the cars they manufactured, not only on installments, but at a reduced cost. The idea was that the more Ford cars on the road, the better it would be for business. Ford was correct. With the success of mass production, the cost of the car came down and Americans were able to buy the Model T in the millions. In a nod to customer satisfaction, Henry Ford quipped, "They can buy the car in any color, as long as it's black."

This corporate paternalism was prevalent across industries and greatly benefited workers. However, workers still had very little say in the speed of production or in how personnel should be managed. Workers wanted to be more self-determinant, but that was not the thinking of those in charge. Anti-unionism was also a key feature of paternalism. Henry Ford was also a leader in this regard. Even discussing unionization in a Ford plant was grounds for dismissal. Throughout the 1920s, Ford and others like him were determined to make unionism a thing of the past.

Another notion that many in the early years of the 1920s wanted to relegate to the past was open immigration. Over the course of the previous three decades, immigration from southern and eastern Europe exploded. Italians, Greeks, Russian Jews, and various Eastern Europeans flooded into the cities of the United States. They did provide a cheap labor pool, but they were also seen as dramatically altering the culture of the United States. Unlike the previous large group of immigrants, the Irish, they didn't speak English and were largely ignorant of representative government. Though the Irish were Catholic, the more folky and superstitious brand of Catholicism brought by these new groups seemed completely alien, even to the church hierarchy, dominated by the Irish. Add to that a strong belief that ideas such as communism and socialism were born and bred in Eastern Europe and the notion of being the "great melting pot" had lost its appeal to many Americans.

In 1922 the US government passed a bill severely restricting the amount of people immigrating to the United States. The law stipulated that no more than two percent of the 1890 population of an ethnic group could immigrate to the United States. The year 1890 was specifically chosen because it was right before the largest waves of immigration arrived. So, if there were 10,000 Italian-Americans in the United States, no more than 200 were allowed to enter the United States in any given year. What once was a mighty stream of new people arriving on the shore of America was slowed to a trickle during the 1920s.

One group in particular seized on the rejection of radical ideas and the rejection of the other. The Ku Klux Klan experienced a great revival in the 1920s. It did take some of its symbolism and tactics from the first rendition of the Klan, but it was a much larger enterprise in the 1920s. The early Klan was almost completely dedicated to the suppression of African-Americans in the southern states. The new Klan was no friend of African-Americans but was also decidedly nativist. It was anti-immigrant, anti-Jewish and anti-Catholic. Its membership extended well outside of the South with its largest membership in Indiana. The original Klan was much more secretive than its successor. Klansmen publicly ran for office and held various governmental posts. It wasn't the racist and xenophobic rhetoric of the Klan that led to their demise, but the conviction of their leader in Indiana on rape and murder charges. Though the Indiana Klan considered itself independent of the national organization, the terrible crime along with the level of corruption exposed by the trial seriously crippled the influence of the Ku Klux Klan by the end of the decade as participants in local and national elections.

The Ku Klux Klan revival demonstrated that nativist ideas were popular across the country, but one of the most polarizing events that also demonstrated the internal conflict of the United States was the trial of two Italian immigrants, Nicola Sacco and Bartolomeo Vanzetti. In 1920, a clerk and security guard from a shoe company was killed and robbed of the company's payroll, about $15,000, in Braintree, Massachusetts, close to Boston. Witnesses said that two Italian-looking men had perpetrated the crime. Authorities searched for suspects, especially one named Mario Buda. The police were alerted that Buda, along with his friends Sacco and Vanzetti, was in a garage to pick up his car after some repairs. The police arrived after the men had already left but managed to catch up with Sacco and Vanzetti and arrest them for the robbery and murder.

The vague description of Italian men was enough for the Braintree police to suspect the two men, and after questioning, Sacco and

Vanzetti were caught in a number of inconsistencies and lies. More alarming and damning was that searches of both of the prisoners' residences revealed anarchist literature, though both claimed not to be anarchists. Coupled with the fact that both had lied about owning weapons, including a pistol similar to the one used to commit the murders, an indictment was issued, and a trial was set.

Much of the trial centered on the material evidence surrounding the case, what guns did Sacco and Vanzetti possess and when did they actually own them, could any witnesses positively identify the men. The prosecution did not actively push the anarchist connection. Sacco and Vanzetti, however, did. The presiding judge charged the jury not to consider the defendants' political leanings, but it is hard to imagine that they didn't come under consideration. The jury only deliberated for three hours before returning a guilty verdict.

The trial of Sacco and Vanzetti could have remained an obscure, local trial. One of the defense attorneys, Fred Moore, however, spoke out about the trial and made the claim that the two men were convicted because of their political beliefs and were only arrested because of the ethnic biases of a corrupt police force. After this storyline gained traction first across the country then around the world, left-leaning citizens and radicals began protesting and raising funds for Sacco's and Vanzetti's appeals.

The legal maneuverings around the Sacco and Vanzetti case took six years to resolve. In all of their appeals, the convictions were upheld. In 1925, another man confessed to the murders, but it was not enough to convince the court to grant a new trial. After all of the possible appeals were exhausted, including a request for a pardon from the governor of Massachusetts, Sacco and Vanzetti were executed on August 22, 1927.

Their deaths were greeted with large protests around the world. Over 10,000 mourners attended their funeral. There were bombings in various cities as acts of protest against their executions. For many, the trial and execution of Sacco and Vanzetti was evidence of a corrupt system that was set against any liberal, let alone radical, thought. The truth of the matter is a little more complicated as the years have passed. There is some evidence that Sacco actually participated in the crimes. In 1961, a forensics test demonstrated that the gun used in the murders was the same gun owned by Sacco. While there is some doubt about the 1961 test, the debate surrounding the case in the 1920s has endured as an example of how divided the nation was concerning both radical politics and immigrants.

Radicalism wasn't only feared in socio-economic circumstances. Concurrent with the trials of Sacco and Vanzetti, a trial in Tennessee also captivated audiences around the nation. John Thomas Scopes substituted in a biology class and proceeded to teach some of the fundamentals of evolutionary theory. In doing so, he violated a state law in Tennessee which prohibited the teaching of evolution in any state-funded school. Scopes was indicted and brought to trial in July of 1925.

It is probably the most covered trial of a crime that carried a fine of only $100. It was more about showcasing the scientific facts against the religious beliefs. Scopes set out to challenge the law and intentionally be brought to trial. As the trial date approached, the story quickly went from a local one to a national one. The local lawyers were all but shoved aside as Clarence Darrow, the most famous lawyer of the era, came in to argue for the defense while William Jennings Bryan presented for the prosecution. Along with the famous lawyers arguing the case, the most famous journalist of the generation, H.L. Menken, covered the proceedings for *The Baltimore Sun*. Menken gave the trial its name, the Monkey Trial. It was also the first trial to be broadcast on radio with WGN from Chicago capturing every moment of the trial.

The trial reached absurd levels when Darrow called his rival, Jennings Bryan, to the stand. It was the showcase of the trial as Darrow questioned and prodded Jennings Bryan about the intricacies of faith and presented how it did not stand up to scientific inquiry.

Much of this exchange is dramatically recounted in the award-winning play (and later film), *Inherit the Wind*.

After Bryan's examination, the judge ruled that the entire testimony was irrelevant to the proceedings and the jury shouldn't consider it. Ultimately, Scopes was found guilty, but was cleared on appeal. He did not win his appeal because of the argument between religion and science, but on a legal technicality. Though the trial is often seen as a triumph of reason over tradition, the guilty verdict also highlights that many Americans were not ready for such a radical step in their thinking or education.

Chapter 3 – Old Causes Finishing Business

Many causes and events of the 1920s were a reaction to what many saw as radical changes to what the fabric of America was. The ideas of an earlier era, of the Progressives, seemed far too disruptive after World War One. Radical politics, massive immigration, and new scientific and social ideas were no longer as welcome as they had been in 1913.

Two social movements for the Progressive period reached their apex in 1920, namely women's suffrage and prohibition. Both movements had their modern founding in the middle of the nineteenth century. Both were tied to middle-class women and the mores of evangelical religion. Both were often cast as not only good for society, but as a remedy for some of the worst aspects of society that seemed to be increasing with each passing year. Both grew to massive movements that eventually swelled into millions of supporters. Both movements were committed to their respective causes and worked for decades to finally see their goals achieved in 1920. Only one, however, lasted. The other would become a deadly national farce that quite possibly did more harm than good.

The Seneca Falls Convention of 1848 in the Finger Lakes Region of Upstate New York is considered the beginning of the modern women rights movement. Lucretia Mott and Elizabeth Cady Stanton organized the meeting to discuss the major cause of the day, the abolition of slavery (they even had Frederick Douglass as a speaker), but they also were determined to start the discussion of women's political rights, specifically the right to vote.

After the Civil War and the official end to slavery, many in the abolition movement receded from politics. Stanton and Mott were not among them. The cause of women's suffrage became their prominent focus. With another ally, Susan B. Anthony, they took a page from the abolitionist movement and began publishing a weekly newspaper, *The Revolution*, to publicize and campaign for women's rights. In addition, various groups dedicated to women's rights were created in the postwar landscape. The National Woman Suffrage Association and the American Woman Suffrage Association were the most prominent. The latter included other prominent women's voices such as Lucy Stone and Julia Ward Howe. Though the groups were often rivals, both of their activities and activism furthered the cause of a woman's right to vote.

Concurrent with the beginnings of the women's suffrage movement, another social movement began, gathering membership from many of the same places. The temperance movement, like the women's movement, sprang from the same halls and churches as the abolition movement did before the Civil War. Like the women's movement, the temperance movement continued after the war was over and became the focal point for many activists. A number of temperance organizations were founded across the country, but the most prominent, the Women's Christian Temperance Union (WTCU), began in 1875. The organization's most prominent leader, Frances Willard, became its president in 1879. While the battle against alcohol was always at the forefront of the WTCU's campaigns, Willard steered the group into such causes as women's suffrage, labor rights, and children's rights.

These two movements grew and matured together and were largely seen as women's causes. Suffrage, naturally, was the main concern, but temperance was as well because it was seen as a means of protecting the family from the ravages of a drunken father and husband. The thinking was that by having women vote and have influence on policy, they could curb some of the most destructive and corrupt tendencies of the male-dominated world of politics.

Both movements borrowed from the tactics of their abolitionist predecessors, namely trying to influence government policy through petitioning state and federal officials. The women's movement engaged in a more piecemeal approach, attempting to affect the suffrage rules of western territories as they became states. In many western territories, women already could vote because the number of women was so sparse in the West that allowing them the right to vote seemed inconsequential to the presiding territory, later state governments. The western region has historically been more liberal regarding social mores. As the recent legalization of the marijuana movement demonstrates, western states are more willing to test new policies.

The women's movement met with success across the West as states allowed women to vote in 1893 through 1896. The temperance movement did not employ the same methods. Instead, the temperance movement of the nineteenth century was identified with large meetings and demonstrations, culminating in the Women's Crusade in 1873-1874, a series of large marches throughout much of the Midwest, made famous by Timothy Shay Arthur's book, *Women to the Rescue*. In the 1890s, like the suffrage movement, the temperance movement started to look to local politics as a means to change alcohol laws, eventually leading to national prohibition, a concept that wasn't seen as a realistic goal until their first true lobbying group began, the Anti-Saloon League (ASL).

The ASL was founded in 1893 and quickly became the most vocal supporter of national prohibition. It eventually eclipsed the WCTU. By the turn of the century, the ASL was pressuring various politicians from local officials to congressmen and senators to vote for their cause. The Anti-Saloon League publicized its successes through the copious amounts of literature it produced from its publishing house, The American Issue. One of the highlights of their annual report were the county-by-county maps the ASL created showing which counties were dry and touted the gain in dry counties from year to year.

The temperance movement had a flair for the dramatic even into the twentieth century. One of the most flamboyant demonstrators against alcohol was Carrie (Carry A) Nation. Often pictured with a hatchet, the Missouri native became known for entering saloons, famous hatchet in hand. After praying in the barroom, Nation took her ax and destroyed as much of the bar as she could. She toured through much of the Midwest, conducting the same behavior from town to town. Nation was arrested over 30 times but that did not deter her zeal for the prohibition cause. Though not part of the Anti-Saloon League, her destructive theatrics made the measured political approach of the league much more appealing to many supporters.

As the twentieth century progressed, both movements gained momentum. In 1910, the state of Washington granted women the right to vote. More and more industries saw the benefit of a sober workforce and started to support prohibition legislation. Furthermore, the tension between the rural and urban areas was increasing. The nativist stock of the country saw the immigrant-filled cities as the main example of the ill effects of drinking. Combined with the strengthening evangelicalism of the early twentieth century with preachers and the call within progressive politics for reform, prohibition started to look like a real possibility. Also looking like a matter of if and not when was women's suffrage. Between 1911 and 1914, seven states gave women the right to vote. As women marched in the largest suffrage demonstration ever in Washington DC in 1913, there was a confidence in both the suffrage movement and the prohibition movement that wasn't present a generation earlier.

World War One helped both movements reach their zeniths by 1920. When President Wilson authorized the draft to build the nation's army, the labor shortage it created was significant. In record numbers, middle-class women, those same women that were agitating for the right to vote, went to work. Almost all arguments against women being able to cast a vote were discounted. During the war and in the immediate postwar years, women marched in front of the White House urging President Wilson to join their cause. They echoed the same rhetoric that Wilson used regarding the war. If the United States was truly a beacon of democracy to the world, then shouldn't all of its citizens have the right to vote? In October of 1918, the president came out in support of equal suffrage, and the following May, the Susan B. Anthony Amendment was proposed. After making its way through the House and Senate, it was finally ratified by the states in August of 1920.

The route of the prohibition movement was a bit more circuitous, but the end was eventually the same. In order to preserve grain for the domestic and military food supply, prohibition was national policy during World War One. The same year that the wartime prohibition went into effect, Congress proposed the Eighteenth Amendment, banning the manufacture, sale, or transportation of intoxicating liquors. The bill sailed through the House and Senate and was ratified by the states in eleven months on January 29, 1919. One year from that date, the new amendment and corresponding legislation would go into effect. The ASL and WCTU were triumphant and sure that a new age of peace and prosperity was on hand for the United States.

Chapter 4 – The Cost of Prohibition

The passage of two constitutional amendments in one year was practically unheard of in US history. Other than the Bill of Rights and the Reconstruction amendments, changes to the Constitution came slowly, if at all. Two of the great social causes of the latter half of the nineteenth and early twentieth century had reached fruition. The cause of women's suffrage would not be retracted in the ensuing years. The idea of repealing the Nineteenth Amendment seems ludicrous to modern sensibilities. Though the fight for total equality for women continues, taking away the right to vote is preposterous.

Amazingly, it is equally preposterous to modern thinking that there was ever a time where there was a complete ban on alcohol in the United States. People wonder how did lawmakers ever think that prohibition was a good idea? What were they thinking?

That has been the question historians have been trying to answer almost since the Eighteenth Amendment was repealed in 1933. One of the first answers to these questions revolves around the perceived popularity of prohibition. Lawmakers from the federal to the most local level were overwhelmingly in favor of prohibition. Many took this stance out of fear of reprisal from the ASL and their very effective pressure techniques to ensure compliance with their agenda. So as the amendment made its way through Congress then the statehouses across the nation, many policymakers were sure that the enforcement of the amendment wouldn't be a great challenge since, at least according to the number the ASL provided, the people wanted this amendment.

Along these same lines, many people saw prohibition as something for other people to worry about. The strongest support for the amendment came from rural areas of the nation and the amendment was seen as a means to clean up the vices of the city, especially the immigrant and working-class areas of the cities, since these were seen as the worst parts of any given urban area. Similarly, the middle and upper-class people of the cities saw prohibition as a way to clean up the worst part of their cities. Prior to when the law went into effect, many upper-class citizens bought a great deal of alcohol to stock in their cellars. It may be good for the nation as a whole to go dry, but that shouldn't preclude having wine at dinner. Interestingly, when it came to enforcing prohibition, the federal government had much more success in rural areas than it ever did in urban ones.

It was this hubris that contributed to the lack of funding given to the enforcement of prohibition. Up until the Nineteenth Amendment, federal oversight over any single program was more the exception than the rule. To that end, only about $500,000 was spent on prohibition enforcement in 1923. Only 1,500 agents were created within the new Prohibition Bureau (at first housed in the IRS) to enforce the law for the entire nation.

What's more, the Volstead Act, the congressional act that actually created the laws to govern prohibition, was confusing and seemed contradictory at times. There were numerous exceptions to the law. Homebrewing was considered legal, and it was illegal to search private homes for alcohol. There were exceptions made for religious practices and the American Medical Association lobbied for an exception for doctors in order to prescribe alcohol if needed. Considering the small number of agents, the amount of exemptions to the law, and the vast amounts of territory that were expected to be covered, it is amazing that Prohibition agents caught anyone at all.

The exploits of some of the agents became legendary, if not comical. Prohibition agents Isidore "Izzy" Einstein and Moe Smith focused more on the spectacle of an arrest than of bringing about justice. Einstein and Smith would don elaborate costumes to infiltrate illegal drinking establishments and spring on the patrons at the proper moment for dramatic effect. In at least one case, the ruse was so impressive the people at the club applauded Einstein and Smith for their wonderful display. In keeping with the spirit of their approach to enforcing the law, it was common knowledge that after making a significant bust, Einstein and Smith enjoyed a beer or cocktail to unwind.

The whimsy of Einstein and Smith aside, the reality of prohibition had a much darker side. There is a prevailing belief that organized crime didn't start in the United States until the 1920s. One look at the history of the late nineteenth century dispels that notion. The various Tenderloin districts in cities such as Chicago and New York are a testament to the ability of criminals to organize their money-making endeavors. The prohibition of alcohol just gave those same organizations, and some new ones, a great opportunity to make a lot of money. When it comes to substantial money and criminals, violence is sure to follow.

The most famous location of such a vortex of money, corruption, and violence was the city of Chicago. The demand for alcohol was great in the city and many crime organizations were more than happy to oblige. In Chicago, this meant that control of the city's South Side went to the predominantly Italian-American gang, headed by Johnny Torio and Al Capone. The North Side of the city was controlled by the predominantly Irish-American gang, headed by Dean O'Banion. With so much money at stake, a bloody war between the two gangs was inevitable. The murder rate in Chicago spiked. O'Banion was one of the many casualties, shot in his flower shop in 1924. Though the murder victims were almost exclusively gang members, the public perception was that the city was unsafe. In 1929, the most famous murders of all cemented Chicago's reputation as the murder capital of the world.

The St. Valentine's Day Massacre occurred in Chicago's North Side. It was an attempt to kill the current leader of the North Side gang, Bugs Moran. The murderers, disguised as policemen, probably saved

Moran's life that day. As he was approaching the place where the murders would occur, Moran noticed a police presence and made a hasty exit. Many of his fellow gangsters weren't so lucky. The members of the North Side Gang were lined up along a wall and gunned down without prejudice. Even at the time it was largely known that Al Capone had ordered the hit, but there was little proof that he was involved. No matter; with Moran's operation severely hampered, Capone had unprecedented control of the city.

The brutality of the St. Valentine's Day Massacre was the type of crime and violence that prohibition was supposed to stop. Two years before the massacre, in an attempt to bring justice to the Midwestern metropolis, the Bureau of Prohibition (now part of the Treasury Department) sent one of its top agents, Eliot Ness to specifically take on Capone. Ness had some success in hurting Capone's illegal liquor operations, but not enough to put a real dent in Capone's business. As the St. Valentine's Day Massacre revealed, Capone was still able to carry out even the most brutal of actions. At least through the 1920s, Al Capone was truly untouchable.

While many similar events soured public opinion on prohibition, the St. Valentine's Day Massacre convinced many former allies of prohibition that the great social experiment was a failure. A longtime ally to the ASL and the prohibition cause, many Republicans now started to rethink their position. Women, also a stalwart ally to the prohibition movement, began to divide along the issue as well. By the end of the decade, what had seemed like a decided issue in 1920 was an open debate during the presidential election of 1928.

The cultural feelings toward alcohol also shifted during the 1920s. The brutal reality of World War One made many doubt whether drinking or not was a particularly pressing issue anymore. When compared to the world's problems, the concern over people having a drink or two seemed naive and out of date.

This was especially the case when it came to women. With the passage of the Nineteenth Amendment, the idea of the "New

Woman" became popular around the country. One of the iconic images of the decade, the flapper, illustrates this new idea of womanhood. A young, energetic woman partaking in a nightlife that had been almost exclusively male was a powerful message. The flapper was often pictured in a short dress, at times smoking a cigarette or holding a cocktail glass. She wore makeup, and while in the company of men was seen as independent. This was in stark contrast to the image of the women who campaigned against alcohol, with their Victorian dresses and stern looks. Ironically, the stuffy, buttoned-up women who worked against alcohol also worked equally hard for the right to vote, which signaled the beginning of this new era.

Chapter 5 – A New World

The flapper wasn't just a symbol for women of the 1920s; it also sums up the idea that the 1920s brought something new to American culture. The postwar world of the United States saw a great deal of innovations and changes that were not even considered before the war. From popular and mass culture to sports and higher culture, the idea of "the new" was at the forefront of American thought and culture.

Along with the flapper, no single invention signified the changing landscape of America more than the automobile. Though invented in the 1890s, it wasn't until Henry Ford and his mass production and distribution of cars made them ubiquitous throughout the country. The car became a symbol of independence and freedom. Railroads were still the preferred method of travel over long distances and airplanes were still exotic, but cars offered a way to travel fast, enclosed, and relatively cheap.

The enclosed feature was especially significant because of the amount of privacy offered, especially in the backseat. The emergence of dating in the 1920s was a significant cultural turning point in the United States. What had before occurred in a more structured and supervised environment became an activity that could escape parental supervision, especially in a car.

Cars didn't just alter personal behavior, but their production created a boom in industries across the economy. Rubber manufacturing transformed the city of Akron and the demand for steel kept the plants in cities like Chicago, Cleveland, and especially Pittsburgh humming right along. Dirt roads were no longer a viable alternative and the brick streets of many cities were not ideal for automobiles. Road construction throughout the United States was a priority for many cities and states.

Though the oil business had been in existence since the late nineteenth century, the advent of the automobile offered a major boost to its revenue. Not only was oil needed as a lubricant for the engines and axles of cars, but after a process of refinement, crude oil could be rendered as gasoline which provided the fuel for cars. The relationship between all of these industries, steel, oil, rubber, along with glass, paint and others, revolved to some degree around the production of automobiles. It was the beginning of an American economy that dominated the world later in the twentieth century.

The ascension of cars wasn't the only culturally significant change of the 1920s. The golden age of radio was also during this decade. News events were broadcast through various stations, but entertainment as well. Music was the most popular format, including Live from the Grand Ole Opry and National Barn Dance featured on WLS in Chicago. Orchestras were broadcast as well. Mysteries and comedies were part of the daily makeup of radio programming. The explosion of radio stations and the amount of money spent on radios between 1921-1927 demonstrates how popular the new technology had become in a relatively short time.

Cultural assimilation was also achieved radio programming. There were many foreign language broadcasts for communities to tune into, but the larger, more commercial stations were also popular among the ethnic neighborhoods of cities. It is telling that the first radio soap opera didn't center on a white middle or upper-class protagonist. Instead, it centered on the stories of an ethnic family living in New York. *The Goldbergs* was a huge hit and a cultural phenomenon that was later recast as one of the first television shows as well.

Another important part of radio's appeal, especially to immigrant communities, was the playing of music. Much of the classical music played was known by immigrant families, and in cases of German and Italian families, broadcast operas were not only entertainment but points of pride. Ethnic groups heard their language being broadcast to everyone across the nation.

Radio was the main technology to make its way into the American home in the 1920s, but another innovation got people out of their homes—moving pictures. Movies, like automobiles, had been more of a curiosity before World War One. Nickelodeons on boardwalks or perhaps special occasions like the world fairs featured moving pictures, but the movie theater didn't come into its own until after the war. This was due to the fact that the holder of many of the patents on movie-making equipment was Thomas Edison, who was very selective at who could use his materials.

The main solution to this problem was for production companies to get as far away from Edison as they could. Studios started moving out to California in the 1910s, and by the 1920s, all of the major motion picture studios were located in Hollywood. Not only was it financially better for producers to be in Hollywood, the milder climate enabled film producers to make movies year-round. Actors from the silent movies became national stars, another spectacle that had almost exclusively been reserved for politicians and preachers. Douglas Fairbanks Sr., Mary Pickford, Lillian Gish, and Rudolph Valentino all became household names through their popular movies.

In 1927, an experiment by Warner Brothers Studio paid huge dividends for the company. In that year they produced the first film to feature sound, *The Jazz Singer*, starring Al Jolson. Though much of the dialogue was still rendered on dialogue cards throughout the film, the singing by Jolson was audible. Other studios were skeptical of the new technology until they saw the overwhelming success of *The Jazz Singer*. The shift from silent pictures to talkies redefined Hollywood.

The story of *The Jazz Singer*, the son of an immigrant struggling with being true to his heritage versus wanting to be a part of America, was familiar to many first-generation immigrants and ethnic communities. Movies were the most accessible form of American entertainment to the ethnic communities of the American city. Immigrants and their children didn't go to the movies in the large movie palaces of the downtown districts like Times Square in New York or State Street in Chicago, but to the small storefront theaters in their neighborhood. However, with the advent of sound, the expense of retrofitting a theater was prohibitive to ethnic owners. While still not regular patrons, immigrant families went to larger and more commercial theaters to see the latest movies.

The door had been shut on immigrants at the beginning of the decade and there was a fear among ethnic leaders that the lack of new arrivals would lessen the connection to the "old country" for many in their communities. In some ways, this turned out to be the case. An interesting hybrid occurred. More and more immigrants were branching out, like the Jazz Singer, and exploring the new culture of the 1920s, but the ethnic communities that had been established over the course of the early years of the twentieth century were still strong. Distinct enclaves dotted cities all over the United States. Chicago is often called the city of neighborhoods, but those neighborhoods were established by various groups. Bridgeport was Irish, Little Italy was Italian, Maxwell Street was Jewish, and so on. These neighborhood boundaries lasted well past the 1920s, even as many in the communities were experiencing the rest of the city with the other ethnic groups it shared spaces.

Other leisure activities were getting people out of their homes along with movies. Spectator sports saw a dramatic rise in attendance during the 1920s, none more so than the national pastime, baseball.

One person brought the most attention to the sport, George Herman Ruth, better known as Babe.

Baseball was in need of a new hero. The 1919 World Series was under suspicion of being fixed. The American League team, the Chicago White Sox, were rumored to have taken money from gamblers in New York in order to sabotage the series. By 1920, a grand jury was called and indictments were being handed down. Though the players were acquitted in the courts, the new commissioner of baseball, Kenesaw Landis, banned the eight players suspected of taking bribes. The large man from Baltimore with the crazy swing was just what baseball needed to get back to the positive light as America's pastime.

Babe Ruth was born in Baltimore, Maryland and began his Major League career in Boston, but it wasn't until his trade to New York for the 1920 season that he become a major draw for the MLB. That first year in New York, Babe Ruth and the New York Yankees drew over a million fans to the ballpark, a number almost unheard of before 1920. The Yankees continued to draw a million plus for almost every year in the decade, routinely topping the Major League in attendance. It wasn't just in New York either; when the Yankees were in town, attendance jumped for the home team.

People also came to see Babe Ruth and the colossal home runs he routinely hit. No one hit home runs the same way as he did, high, far, and soaring over the fence. Until 1920 and Babe Ruth's new approach to hitting by using an uppercut swing and swinging hard, hitters focused more on spraying the ball to all fields, on contact over power. It wasn't just his home runs either; people loved to see him just swing and miss because it was such a violent action. Ruth often spun himself so hard going for a home run that when he missed, he would fall down. It was baseball meeting slapstick comedy.

The 1920s saw, largely because of Babe Ruth, the emergence of the New York Yankees as the preeminent sports franchise in the United

States. Before the arrival of Ruth, the Yankees were the third team in the city of New York, behind the Brooklyn Dodgers and the New York Giants, the dominant team of the previous decade. The Yankees were tenants of the Giants in their home ballpark, the Polo Grounds. When Babe Ruth was traded to the Yankees, all of that changed. The Yankees outdrew the Giants to the point where the manager and part owner of the Giants, John McGraw, decided not to renew the lease of the American League upstarts.

It didn't matter to the Yankees and their owner, Jacob Ruppert. He had already made plans to build a modern structure in the Bronx. Yankee Stadium was a massive building, constructed across the river from the Polo Grounds. First used in 1923, it would be home to dozens of championships over the ensuing decades, the first one coming the year it opened.

Three years later, the Yankees, with Ruth as part of the batting order, the famed Murderer's Row dominated the American League for the next three years. Though none of the players rivaled Ruth in playing or celebrity, the team's fame is something that many modern teams are still compared to.

The popularity of Ruth went beyond his playing. He was often seen out and about in New York and other cities. He was, like Hollywood actors, a star. More than any other person though, Ruth embodied the 1920s. He was big, loud, and gregarious. The 1920s are often compared to as a party and Ruth was the life of that party.

Rivaling Ruth for popularity as a sports figure was the heavyweight champion, Jack Dempsey. Like Ruth, Dempsey came from a poor background and used sport as a means to make money and get out from harsh circumstances. It wasn't long into his career that Dempsey took the title and held on to it for seven years. As he defended his crown, Dempsey's fights filled the largest stadiums in the United States, for example, 85,000 in New York's Polo Grounds. Even when he was no longer the champ, his rematch against Gene Tunney drew over 100,000 spectators and over $2 million in gate receipts. Millions more listened to the fight on the radio. The infamous "Long Count Fight" was thought to be the most watched sporting event in history. (Dempsey lost in a decision.)

In addition to baseball and boxing, a relatively new game, largely associated with the upper-class environs of the college and university, started to make its presence known. College football was quite popular with stars like Red Grange playing for the University of Illinois and the Four Horsemen of Notre Dame filling stadiums and headlines across the country. In 1920, a new venture was started in Canton, Ohio. A group of fourteen teams started professional football. In 1922, the league would adopt the name, the National Football League. Playing in small stadiums and usually renting from baseball teams who were not in season, the league was not much of a rival to the big sports of baseball, boxing, and horse racing. It did begin to attract fans, especially when college stars such as Grange decided to play in the league.

As large as any sports celebrity or movie star was a man who symbolized the rugged individualism that was also prominent in the 1920s. Charles Lindbergh made the first solo flight across the Atlantic Ocean in 1927. The daring feat earned him almost instant worldwide fame. Parades and banquets were held in his honor and he received medals from the US and French governments. He was an individual hero for a decade that celebrated personal greatness. Unlike the earlier Progressive Era, which was about social responsibility and about taking care of those who couldn't take care of themselves, the 1920s was about personal accomplishments. Like Babe Ruth and Jack Dempsey, Lindbergh was a star on his own merits.

Another significant contribution to the culture of the 1920s, one that has endured to help define the era, was writing. Not all of the authors of the time became rich and famous, but many of the most notable did and reflected, like Babe Ruth and Jack Dempsey, the ethos of the age. The most iconic of this generation of writers was F. Scott Fitzgerald.

Fitzgerald, unlike his other famous contemporaries Ruth and Dempsey, came from middle-class means in Minnesota. He attended Princeton and was determined to become a writer. He spent time in the army during World War One, though he never went to Europe on account of the war ending before he could be deployed. His first novel, *This Side of Paradise*, was an immediate success, and he and his wife, Zelda, began living in Paris and New York.

Fitzgerald published four more novels and numerous short stories, but it was his lifestyle with his wife that made him a celebrity. The couple lived in splendor and spent a great deal of money to keep up appearances. His alcohol consumption became an issue even in a time where drinking was often overlooked. Because of this, Fitzgerald was often struggling to make ends meet.

Other writers who spent time in Paris along with Fitzgerald became known as the "Lost Generation." This moniker encapsulates the idea that much of the culture of the 1920s was a reaction to the First World War. The writings of Fitzgerald's contemporary and friend, Ernest Hemingway, dealt explicitly with the meaning of life after such a horrific experience as a modern war. Sinclair Lewis, perhaps the most commercially successful of the generation, was a fierce social critic through his novels, especially *Babbit*. William Faulkner is also part of this generation and his work is as profound as his contemporaries, but from a distinctly different point of view. Unlike the writers from New York and Paris, Faulkner completed much of his writing in the South, especially his home state of Mississippi.

Faulkner and his southern inspiration was more of the exception than the rule of the 1920s. According the United States census for 1920, for the first time more people lived in urban areas than in rural ones. The famous song "How Ya Gonna Keep 'Em Down on the Farm?" was a fitting theme for the entire decade. The nightlife of jazz clubs and speakeasies was in the city. The biggest movie houses and all of the sporting venues were in the city. The 1920s are often called a golden age for sports and music, but it was truly the golden age of the American city.

People demanded the modernity that the city promised. Even if they decided not to move, more and more people in rural areas wanted what the city had, especially electricity. Both inside and outside of the city, people wanted items that required electricity. The system that delivered that power was a key component to the infrastructure to the modern city. This new utility became as important to modern life as clean water and drivable streets. Electricity was a symbol of the new mass consumption that came to define the 1920s.

As social movements and new entertainments emerged in the 1920s, the common denominator for them was the city. Whether celebrating the urban lifestyle or reacting against it, the city, unlike previous generations, was at the center of the American consciousness. Frederick Jackson Turner claimed that the American frontier had closed in 1893, but in the decade following World War One, a new frontier was being explored by more people than ever before, the American city.

Chapter 6 – African-Americans

The history of African-Americans is filled with constant hardship and struggle. Emerging from the horrific circumstances of slavery, only to be quickly reduced to second-class citizens through the forces of Jim Crow, African-Americans have endured more than any race in the United States. That began to change as African-Americans moved to the large cities in the North during and after the First World War. Opportunities for personal prosperity and advancement that African-Americans hadn't seen since the Reconstruction era were within reach in their new surroundings. By 1928, the first African-American since the 1870s was elected to Congress from Chicago, Oscar DePriest. By 1930, forty percent of African-Americans had moved to urban areas. African-Americans were earning more money than ever before and casting ballots that had been denied to them throughout the South.

It wasn't easygoing however. White resentment and fear within those same cities sparked riots and random violence that was all too similar to the threats and intimidation that African-Americans experienced in the South. What's more, the African-Americans already settled in northern cities didn't want the less cultured of their race to upset the delicate balance that they had achieved.

Though it was not as established by law in the North as it was in the South, segregation was the reality of the northern cities. Specific neighborhoods were deemed African-American neighborhoods, and it was almost impossible for any African-American to move from those boundaries. The Hill District in Pittsburgh, Bronzeville in Chicago, and Harlem in New York became the centers for black life and culture throughout the 1920s.

It was that culture that blossomed in the 1920s though, especially from the migrants arriving from the South. If one looks at the spread of jazz music from its roots in New Orleans to its popularity in Kansas City, to Chicago and then across the country in places like New York, it practically follows the migration route of thousands of African-Americans. Two of the most prominent jazz musicians followed this familiar route.

Jelly Roll Morton was born in New Orleans and by the age of fourteen was playing piano in brothels around the city. Soon after he began to tour the South and eventually made his way to Chicago where he first recorded some of his music. Morton claimed to have invented a new style of music called jazz and took his new sound to other cities around the country, especially New York.

Morton may or may not have created jazz, but another son of New Orleans made jazz an international phenomenon. Armstrong was a trumpet player by trade and it was as an instrumentalist that he made his first recordings. His Hot Five and Hot Seven groups which began in Chicago were his earliest successes. Armstrong also became known for his distinctive vocal style. When he sang, it sounded unique, sounding in many ways like his baritone-speaking voice. Unlike many singers of the day, Armstrong didn't try to mimic a falsetto or change his voice in anyway. His voice was his voice. Armstrong's authenticity influenced later singers like Frank Sinatra and Bob Dylan.

The setting for jazz music was the nightclub, usually in the African-American neighborhood of any given city. The most famous of these, the Cotton Club, hosted live music on a nightly basis, and the city's greatest stars like Babe Ruth and Jack Dempsey frequented the famous nightclub. Everyone came to see the most famous and most influential band leader of the era, Duke Ellington.

Duke Ellington was a musician, composer, manager, and pioneer of jazz. His first residency at the Cotton Club has become something of a legend in the history of jazz. Such performers as Bubber Miley and Lonnie Johnson were part of the orchestra that entertained thousands who made the trip to the club over the course of the orchestra's three-year stay. Ellington and his orchestra played for singers, played their own compositions, and provided dance music for the patrons.

These patrons were also something very new to American culture. The audiences at clubs like the Cotton Club were racially mixed. Clubs that catered to a mixed audience were referred to as "black and tans" clubs. These clubs were in the African-American section of cities and whites who attended saw themselves as "slumming." The voyeuristic attitude and atmosphere contributed little to civil rights, but it did demonstrate that there at least might be some openness on social interaction. It was definitely not a push toward equality. African-Americans entertaining whites had been common since the beginning of the nation. However, in the jazz clubs of the 1920s, whites were actually paying for the privilege to be entertained by black artists. In the clubs that were part of the black community, there was no separate dance floor so interaction had to at the very least be tolerated.

The exception to this divided hierarchy were the white musicians who journeyed to these clubs to see musicians play a type of music that inspired them. The young white musicians were not slumming but learning. Famous musicians, such as Hoagy Carmichael, were rebelling against their rural and suburban upbringings and the racial attitudes expressed there. They were not the typical audience member, but since the music had a profound effect on them, later on when they became bandleaders and recording artists, they supported equal rights to African-American musicians and in some cases wouldn't play in clubs that discriminated against some of their players. It is a small example of social change, but significant.

African-Americans and whites sharing a stage was a powerful image that began in the 1920s.

Outside of the United States, another African-American entertainer, Josephine Baker became the one of the most famous Americans in the world. Born in St. Louis, she emigrated to Paris in 1925. She performed throughout Europe, but mostly on the Champs Elysees where the expat community of Americans adored her, especially Ernest Hemingway. Though Baker's debut on Broadway was a failure, over the course of her long career she won over American audiences as well. She was a pioneer in entertainment and used her celebrity to further the cause of civil rights throughout her career.

Dance was also a key import from the South. And as jazz became more and more popular, the dances that were associated with them grew in popularity as well. The Lindy Hop, the Charleston, and the Black Bottom were constantly seen on the dance floors of nightclubs across the nation. The more traditional dances, such as the waltz, were seen as old and out of touch, while the new dances reflected the new times. Young men with slicked back hair held down by pomade and women in short dresses became visible symbols of a generation who were urban, sophisticated, and energetic.

The dance clubs in African-American neighborhoods served a diverse clientele, but many of the businesses in those districts catered to African-Americans. This wasn't because of discrimination on the part of African-American business owners. Since white businesses wouldn't serve black customers, the needs of the community were met by black entrepreneurs. African-Americans started their own insurance companies, funeral parlors, and banks to give other African-Americans the services otherwise denied them. In addition, because white newspapers did not address the issues that concerned the local and national African-American community, black newspapers came to prominence. *The Chicago Defender* and *The Pittsburgh Courier* were two of the largest papers in the black community and had strong circulations outside of their home cities.

Included with these business pioneers were the founders of the first Negro National League, a baseball league made up of players of color which were barred by Major League Baseball. Rube Foster founded the first team, the Chicago Negro Giants, and various cities followed suit with teams of their own. This initial league highlighted some of the best players of the age, including Oscar Charleston and Biz Mackey. Though this first league would not survive the Depression, a new league rose in the 1930s and would last until the late 1950s when integration of baseball was all but complete.

As African-American communities grew and thrived across the United States, one became the epicenter for African-American culture, thought, and political action. Harlem, in New York City, was a symbol to all African-Americans of what their culture was capable of doing. Writers such as Zora Neale Hurston and Langston Hughes were critically acclaimed throughout literary circles.

Harlem is also where African-American political leaders gravitated. A. Philip Randolph, W.E.B. Du Bois, and Marcus Garvey were all active during the 1920s. All three men got their starts in the early part of the twentieth century but met with varying degrees of success in the 1920s. Du Bois was heavily influenced by the experience of African-American soldiers in World War One. After the war, he interviewed many returning African-American soldiers and discovered that those who served were primarily regulated to menial labor. Very few were even issued weapons. Despite this, Du Bois was impressed with the new confidence that many of the returning soldiers had. This new outlook became known as the "New Negro," or the attitude of African-Americans to be more outspoken and vocal for their rights.

As he had been earlier in the century, Du Bois was mostly interested in the integration of African-Americans and whites in US society. After World War One, Du Bois became interested in the concept of Pan-Africanism, the idea that all people descended from the continent of Africa had not only a common background, but a common goal of acceptance and equality around the world. As Du

Bois aged, his Pan-Africanism grew into a more socialist, anti-colonial belief system that defined much of his later writings.

At the second Pan-African Congress, Du Bois met another African-American leader who would challenge Du Bois on a number of his goals within United States society. Marcus Garvey, a Jamaican, was influenced by Booker T. Washington. Though Washington believed in the separation of races on an economic level, Garvey went a step further and called for black separatism, with the ultimate goal voiced in Garvey's Back to Africa movement. The idea behind this movement was that all of the peoples of Africa that had been taken from their ancestral home by the force of slavery should return to Africa and build a new society there. Through his Universal Negro Improvement Association (UNIA), Garvey promoted this goal and the philosophy of Pan-Africanism as well.

In order to further this agenda, Garvey instituted two initiatives. First, the UNIA did as much as it could to promote its cause by celebrating African culture. The organization held almost weekly parades through Harlem, filled with pageantry and military dress to demonstrate the diversity and power of Africans from around the world. It was very much in keeping with the idea of the New Negro, of standing up and being recognized. No event did more to further that cause, however, than when the UNIA held a rally at Madison Square Garden. 25,000 people filled the arena in a celebration of Pan-Africanism.

As might be expected, Du Bois was not an admirer of Garvey and his policy of separatism. In a series of articles in *The Crisis* (the magazine of the NAACP), Du Bois referred to Garvey as the "most dangerous enemy to the Negro race in America and the World." Garvey's reputation wasn't helped when he held a meeting with the leader of the Ku Klux Klan in 1922, stating that the KKK was a better friend to Africans than the many hypocritical whites who claimed to help, but in truth had no desire to do so. Though Garvey's thoughts would be echoed in later years, it did little to gain him supporters and made potential allies, like Du Bois, into adversaries.

The return to Africa wasn't just a theory either. In 1919, the UNIA purchased two ocean liners to begin the process of taking goods and eventually people back to Africa. The Black Star Line, the name given to the company, had a number of problems almost from the beginning and eventually ceased operations by 1922. Adding insult to injury, the Bureau of Federal Investigation took an interest in the company almost immediately and later charged Garvey with mail fraud. He was found guilty and served five years in prison. Upon his release in 1927, Garvey was deported back to Jamaica.

Between the two pillars of Du Bois and Garvey stood the figure of Asa Philip Randolph. As a labor organizer, the beginnings of his greatest successes started in the 1920s. He was a strong supporter of socialism and saw it as the main way to achieve equality for African-Americans specifically, but for all workers more generally.

In 1917 Randolph organized the elevator operators in New York City into a union, and in 1919 he was elected president of the National Brotherhood of Workers of America, a union bringing together African-American dock workers in Virginia. The American Federation of Labor (AFL) pressured the group into disbanding because they felt it was redundant with what they were trying to accomplish with the Longshoremen's union.

Randolph is best known for the union he helped to create, the Brotherhood of Sleeping Car Porters in 1925. There was nothing comparable for the AFL to object to, so the predominantly African-American membership continued to organize. The early years of the union were not particularly successful, as a threatened strike needed to be abandoned because of rumors of strikebreakers being in position to take the union members' jobs. By not following through with the strike, the Brotherhood saw a major decline in its membership. It wouldn't be until the presidency of Franklin Roosevelt and the New Deal that the union would see significant progress in the rights and working conditions of its members.

In spite of the harsh racism that was part of American society in the 1920s, with legal segregation in the South and de facto segregation in the North, African-Americans saw significant gains as a group. A far greater percentage of African-Americans had moved out of the South and were taking better opportunities, even if that meant moving into new cities and creating tensions between them and the whites and established African-American residents For the first time since Reconstruction, African-Americans demonstrated real political and economic power. African-American artists, especially in music, were not just transforming cities, but the national landscape of what American music truly was. Numerous African-American leaders continued to strive for improvements for African-Americans within or perhaps outside of the overall society. This last point continued to be a debate within the ongoing struggle for civil rights.

Chapter 7 – Politics and Policies

The 1920s are remembered as a time of big businesses making substantial profits and the US government supporting those enterprises. As Calvin Coolidge famously said, "The business of America is business." As far as the presidency was concerned in the 1920s, it was the job of the president to promote businesses and stay out of their way as much as possible.

After the First World War and the peace negotiations that followed, a huge shift occurred in the national government. For the first time in a decade, the Republican Party regained the House and the Senate. The midterm elections of 1918 were a bellwether. Voters announced that they were finished with the Progressive agenda that had dominated the first two decades of the twentieth century. Furthermore, it was a clear sign that Americans were finished with Woodrow Wilson's leadership. As the negotiations at Versailles concluded, a backlash against the globalism that Wilson supported was beginning.

The most obvious rejection of American intervention in foreign matters came as the United States Senate rejected the treaty that would have made them members of the League of Nations. The idea of an international body to help govern and solve disputes was one of the signature items of Woodrow Wilson's Fourteen Points, the peace outline he presented at Versailles. By rejecting the League, the Senate was rejecting Wilson's plan for democracy around the globe.

In the fall of 1919, Woodrow Wilson suffered a major stroke and was virtually incapacitated for much of the remainder of his presidency. His wife, Edith, handled much of the day-to-day tasks of the office of the president. She also controlled access to the president. She even doubted members of the president's own party and what they would do if they found out Wilson's condition. He made almost no public appearances or statements. Even so, Wilson needed to be talked out of running for a third term for the presidency.

Warren G. Harding defeated the Democratic nominee, James Cox, with a staggering number of electoral votes, 401 of a possible 531, and an overwhelming percentage of the popular vote, 60.2%. Harding's message which he proclaimed as a "Return to Normalcy" resonated with voters across all demographics and regional areas. The concurrent congressional races added to the Republican majorities in the House and Senate. For the remainder of the decade, all elected branches of the government were dominated by the Republican Party.

Harding was a pretty much a career politician from Ohio, building a strong newspaper until being elected to the Ohio House of Representatives. Though he lost a bid to be governor of the state, he was one of the first senators to be elected under the provisions of the Seventeenth Amendment. As a demonstration of a much different era, Harding barely left Ohio as he campaigned for president, using the "front porch" campaign style also used by past Republican William McKinley.

Harding famously said, "I have no trouble with my enemies. I can take care of my enemies all right. But my damn friends...They're the ones that keep me walking the floor nights!" Harding's administration was riddled with scandals. The most famous of these involved his Secretary of the Interior, Albert Fall. It stemmed from the granting of oil drilling rights in reserves that had been set aside for the US Navy. After the lands were opened for commercial drilling, one parcel in Elk Hills, California and the other in Teapot

Dome, Wyoming, two different oil companies that had paid Fall $400,000 were awarded the leases.

Other scandals also involving illicit payments with the office of the Attorney General and the Department of Veteran Affairs dogged Harding's reputation, but not the man himself. On August 2, 1923 Harding, on a trip to the West Coast, died of a heart attack in San Francisco. Much of the scandal around his administration wasn't revealed until after his death, including his extramarital affairs. At the time of his passing, he was still held in high regard and was still quite popular as president.

Succeeding Harding was his vice president, Calvin Coolidge. When Coolidge died in 1933, noted satirist Dorothy Parker quipped, "How can you tell?" Coolidge may not have been the most expressive of men, but for the better part of the 1920s, he was the President of the United States. His administration shaped policy more than his predecessor and his successor in 1929.

In keeping with the isolationist ideals of the Senate, Coolidge had no plans to enter into any alliance. Though he tried to keep good relations across Europe, his insistence that European nations repay all of their debt did not make for harmony. Germany especially was hard-pressed to repay its reparations costs, but if the United States would not forgive any loan debt—which they did not—other countries had no choice but to continue to insist on keeping Germany's feet to the financial fire.

As noted at the beginning of this chapter, Coolidge was a supporter of big business in the United States. One of the main ways he supported American business, which was conversely detrimental to US relations with other nations, was maintaining high tariffs on imported goods. Five years after the passage of the Fordney-McCumber Tariff, that imposed high tariffs, foreign trading partners began to retaliate and raise their own tariffs on American goods, especially foodstuffs.

Coolidge was dedicated to eliminating the "tyranny of bureaucratic regulation and control." He did little to curb any of the excesses of business that the earlier progressives had tried to control. Overall his policy as far as the federal government was concerned was that the less they did the better. Such policies as child labor and working hour regulations were better left to local and state authorities, not the national government. This was also extended to Wall Street where there was little regulation to begin with; under Coolidge, it was almost nonexistent.

Much in the same vein, Coolidge and his Secretary of the Treasury, Andrew Mellon, believed that lower taxes actually helped the government gain revenue. It was a similar theory as trickle-down economics, wherein the money saved by the wealthy would lead to job creation and growth, thereby making more taxpayers and more revenue for the government. This policy went a considerable way to enriching the already wealthy but did little toward gains of the middle and working class.

Overall though, Americans supported President Coolidge and his policies, especially those that were more protectionist and isolationist. Taxes had been cut and even if the majority of Americans didn't benefit from the cuts, enough did. It all made for a rather predictable 1924 Presidential campaign. It was not quite the landslide of Harding, but it was still a significant win for Coolidge and the Republicans. Coolidge took 382 of a possible 531 electoral votes and received 54% of the popular vote to his Democratic challenger John Davis' total of 28.8%.

Interestingly, one of the constituencies that Coolidge never had a strong relationship with still voted for him. The farmland of the United States, the world's breadbasket, voted solidly for the Republican candidate. The high tariffs especially hurt farmers in the US, especially when other countries raised their tariffs in retaliation. Even if tariffs would have remained low for American goods, American farmers would have still suffered, especially by Coolidge's second term. During and shortly after World War One,

American farmers enjoyed a great boom, feeding the warring nations of the world and those devastated after it. By the mid-1920s, however, Europe was starting to recover. American farms were stuck with a surplus that they could only sell at a loss or not at all. The Coolidge Administration proposed the idea of farming cooperatives as a means to stymie overproduction, but it gained little support.

In the Senate, the Mcnary-Haugen Bill was proposed as a means to aid farmers. The main idea was that the government would buy their surplus production and sell it on the world market. In order to recoup their losses, the government could charge the farmers who benefited from the program and also add sale taxes to food to spread the costs more equitably across other citizens. Coolidge and many on his cabinet opposed the bill, seeing it as too much government interference and not allowing farmers to stand on their own two feet. Both houses of Congress passed the bill, and both times President Coolidge vetoed it. Though the 1920s was in an economic boom for much of the economy, especially by the middle of the decade, farming was hurting quite considerably. Eventually a much more modest bill was proposed and passed in the early days of the Hoover administration.

The election of 1928 saw many of the themes of the previous decade played out. Many assumed that Coolidge would run again, but he declined. Instead the erstwhile Secretary of Commerce, Herbert Hoover, was chosen as the party's candidate. His opposition, Al Smith, split the Democratic Party and brought to bear much of the worst aspects of the 1920s.

Al Smith, Governor of New York, had two issues that caused much dissension between Democrats in urban areas and in the South. First off, Smith was a Roman Catholic, and his religion became a key point throughout the election. Many feared that once elected, the pope would be in control of the United States. Almost solidly Democratic since the Civil War, the South would split when voting in 1928.

Furthermore, an issue that many had thought decided was under debate once again in the campaign of 1928. Smith supported the repeal of prohibition, whereas Herbert Hoover did not. Being from New York and supporting the repeal made those living in rural areas very suspicious of Smith. Adding to that distrust was the fact that many immigrants in urban areas supported Smith.

Supporting an unpopular stance in rural areas, being supported by foreigners, and being a member of a very foreign religion all but doomed Smith's presidential campaign. Hoover, like the two preceding Republican nominees, won handily. He secured 444 electoral votes to Smith's 87, winning all but 7 states. Smith did not even carry his home state of New York. The popular vote wasn't quite as lopsided, with Hoover gaining 58.2% and Smith winning 40.8%. Still, it was a strong support for the policies of the Republican government and a sound rejection of a candidate many believed represented foreign and dangerously anti-American ideas.

In his inaugural address, delivered in March of 1929, Herbert Hoover briefly outlined why he believed he was elected. First, it was because of the preceding years of success, especially the lack of government control in business. Next, by rejecting the anti-prohibitionist, Hoover stated that he felt the nation was demanding that the Eighteenth Amendment be rigorously upheld and enforced. He spoke of improving education and maintaining world peace and concluded on a positive note believing that the best was yet to come.

Chapter 8 – How Did It All End?

Standing before the Capitol Building in the rain during his inauguration on March 4, 1929, Herbert Hoover had full confidence that the future of the country he was about to lead was going to continue on its steady upward trajectory. While there were signs that the economy was slowing, that was acceptable. Hoover was enough of a student of history to realize that there would be setbacks and downturns. Even at the beginning of the decade in the postwar economy there had been struggles. But Hoover believed America and its people would overcome any potential difficulty and come out better than before.

The predicament of farmers was an example of this. A segment of the economy was suffering, but it was not necessarily going to drag the entire economy down along with it. However, there were other industries that were beginning to decline in 1929. Housing construction declined from 1925-1929. Much like farmers, textile manufacturers were hurt by the rebound of Europe after the war, which in turned hurt cotton farmers who had been immune to the difficulties the Midwest was already experiencing.

The conversion economy that of new goods being built and sold to consumers after the war economy had converted to a more domestic focus was also showing signs of slowing down. Many of the goods, like refrigerators and radios, hat people had been buying through the course of the early and mid-1920s were no longer selling at the same rate. By the late 1920s, people were buying less even though production remained high or increased. What's more, wages didn't increase much throughout the decade so households were buying more than ever before on credit. Consumer debt, something almost unheard of in the early part of the twentieth century, was at an all-time high by the end of the 1920s.

Debt was becoming a bit of its own national pastime, namely in the buying and selling of stocks. Speculating on the stock market was something that the middle class especially engaged in during the 1920s. People were investing in the chance of making it big on any stock that looked attractive at the time. In order to do this, many people had to borrow money to invest or buy on margin. In some cases, investors only had to put up 25% of the cost while the broker put up the remaining 75%, or the margin. If the stock went up, and through the 1920s it often did, then everybody won. The broker was paid back his margin with interest and the investor reaped the rest of the profits.

In 1929, as Hoover was taking the oath of office, the stock market was still in an overall climb. There was a dip in that month of March, but shortly after that, it looked like the market would continue to rise as it had done for the previous nine years. Throughout the summer months of 1929, the market continued to climb, reaching its highest level ever in September. Economists were so optimistic that they proclaimed the market had reached a new high plateau.

Circumstances did make some investors nervous. In late September, the London Stock Exchange crashed, making Wall Street reluctant to invest in foreign markets. On October 24th, heavy trading caused the market to fall by 11% initially, but the largest financial institutions in the country pooled their resources and bought large amounts of stock at inflated prices to stabilize the market before it closed that Thursday.

The next day and a half (Wall Street was open for half a day on Saturdays), the market showed signs of recovery. However, on Monday, the opening bell saw another rush to sell and the market plunged and closed down 13%. Much of this was anticipated because investors were facing margin calls to open the week. That is, brokers were asking for the money they had lent investors to make stock purchases. This made the situation only worse though. The next day, known as Black Tuesday, saw the largest number of shares ever traded—16 million. The market closed down another 12%.

The heads of the banks couldn't rally the market this time, especially as the one-two punch of Monday and Tuesday made many want to get out of investing altogether. Investors wanted what money they still had, and they wanted it immediately. This demand for cash created a huge problem for many banks, as they took deposits from customers and had invested them in the market. It didn't take more than a rumor that a bank was about to fail for customers to rush to the bank and demand their money. Though the largest bank runs wouldn't occur until 1930 and 1931, banks were already failing because of smaller panics. In 1929, 650 banks failed. In 1930, that number would double and in 1931 still more banks would close, leaving customers without any recourse. Life savings were lost and mistrust in the financial system would last for generations.

For smaller investors who got out of the market entirely or lost a great deal, spending became much more frugal. This not only affected purchases of household items and larger products, but also spending outside the home on entertainment. Even before 1929, people were spending less. After 1929, the ideal of being a free spender was replaced by being a penny pincher.

The stock market crash is often seen as the abrupt beginning of the Great Depression, but it was much more of a slow boil than an explosion. After the shock of the crash had worn off, many thought the worst was over. It was merely a correction after a decade of unprecedented growth. Like a large stone thrown into a pond, however, the ripples from the crash throughout the economy would make a tenuous situation even worse.

Like many Americans, large corporations invested in the stock market, and like everyone involved in the market, those same corporations lost a great deal of money. Additionally, those companies that were traded on the stock market saw the value of their company stock plummet. What had been a decade of expanding wealth for companies to reinvest and expand their business was now all but dried up.

At first, as companies lost money the first strategy was to finally cut production and limit the hours that employees worked. It wasn't enough to hold off further losses. Even though President Hoover elicited a pledge from many of the largest corporations not to cut jobs, eventually they had little recourse but to do so.

Herbert Hoover was not a cold man, nor was he inept as he is sometimes portrayed. He had very strong Christian beliefs, especially in helping one's fellow man. He was a man of compassion who possessed a strong moral compass and deeply held beliefs. Unfortunately, some of those beliefs were at odds with what was needed to combat the worst economic crisis in world history.

Like most Republicans of his era, he believed strongly in a small federal government. More to the point, he believed the power of the federal government should be used sparingly and not be used to compel people or businesses to do anything. Instead, he believed in volunteerism. As the crisis grew, Hoover called on his fellow Americans to aid one another through the tough times. What made that advice almost comical was that most people were in the same condition as their neighbor. Unemployment rose from 3% in 1928 to 30% by the end of Hoover's term. It is tough to care for one's neighbor when it is almost impossible to care for one's self.

Similarly, Hoover called on churches and other charitable organizations to aid those in need of assistance. Unfortunately, those private organizations were already overwhelmed by requests for help. Neighborhood relief agencies, ethnic aid societies, and mutual aid societies all suffered from a shortage of money and supplies to be able to help all those that came looking for help. In the worst circumstances, some of those same relief agencies were forced to close due to the depression.

Another core belief of Hoover's that was detrimental to the health of the nation was his insistence on keeping a balanced budget. It was his belief that creating a deficit was the wrong choice and would be more detrimental to the people and the nation in the long run. Though the idea of keeping a balanced budget did not waiver, Hoover eventually increased government spending to aid the population.

Ultimately, Hoover and his administration were overwhelmed by the enormity of the depression as it grew. It seemed like every step he took to help did little to nothing. His decision to raise tariffs backfired, as other countries immediately retaliated causing American businesses to face more setbacks. Hoover became more melancholy as the years of his term passed. It was no secret that he was held accountable for the collapse. It is not fair that one person should shoulder all of the blame for the depression, but unfortunately that comes with the office of the President of the United States.

The 1930 midterm elections were a portent of things to come in 1932. Republicans barely held on to a majority in the Senate and lost 52 seats in Congress, making the chamber practically even. The Democrats actually held a one-seat advantage in most votes because of an independent member who leaned more their way. By the 1932 elections, the presidency and Congress were in Democratic control for the first time since the end of World War One. Hoover was out as president and Franklin Roosevelt was in.

Conclusion

The tendency in American history to divide eras by decades is hard to resist. It is a convenient way to mark the time and stay organized when thinking about the past. Unlike most eras, however, the 1920s was a fairly self-contained decade. It is probably better understood as the post-World War One era, but overall the ten years between 1920 and 1929 were unique in American history.

The nation was more urban than rural for the first time in its history and the city became the stage for so much of what was innovative and new during that time. Mass culture came into its own as movies and music drew people from the countryside into the city. They drove in automobiles in record numbers and those cars changed the way cities were designed and had a profound effect on society as a whole. Great celebrities also emerged during the decade because of their larger-than-life deeds and personalities.

For the first time since the Reconstruction, African-Americans made inroads into the political, social, and economic life of the greater United States. They too came to the city looking and finding more opportunities than they had experienced in previous generations. Along with the African-Americans of the Great Migration came their distinctive culture, forever changing the cultural landscape of the United States.

Old causes from the Progressive Era were resolved, but one was a logical conclusion that by the end of the decade would never be questioned. The other seemed antiquated even before the first alcohol stores were destroyed. By 1933, the foregone conclusion of prohibition was reversed and the Eighteenth Amendment was repealed. In the years since, people often wondered why the previous generation ever thought it was a good idea.

However, there were still those who opposed such changes. The Ku Klux Klan experienced a revival after the Reconstruction period, expanding well outside of the southern states. The national government responded to people's fears of European influence and more explicitly immigrants by practically closing the door to those that wanted to enter the United States. The radical ideas of the previous era that gained some traction before World War One were now shunned and feared. To be a radical in the 1920s was to court arrest.

It was a time of great economic expansion, with people buying new products, driving businesses to continue to expand. More people than ever before also invested in the stock market, even if they didn't quite have the money to do so. But money was there to be spent, and the people who lived through the 1920s were more than happy to spend it.

And then, as if on cue, it all came to a dramatic, sudden end befitting the roaring decade. What had been an outwardly focused culture for ten years became a much more inwardly focused one. In many eyes, the American way of life was still viable. Unlike the 1920s, the 1930s would be defined by how Americans banded together and tried to define the American way of life. For many, that meant examining traditions of the past that had fallen out of favor during the 1920s.

Many people have come to see the Great Depression as a reckoning, as a correction for the Jazz Age. History doesn't make those judgments. Suffice it to say; the 1920s were a unique moment in time where change and reaction to those changes were more dramatic than any other time in American history.

Check out more books by Captivating History!

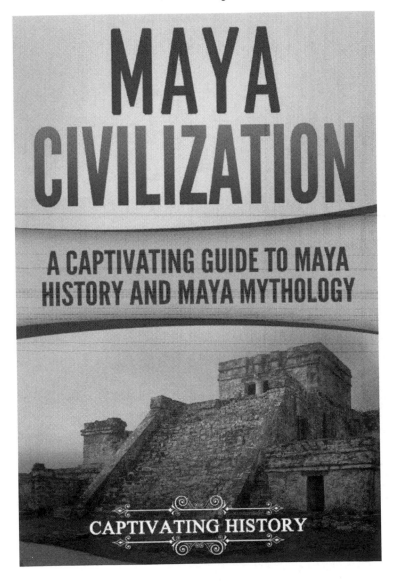

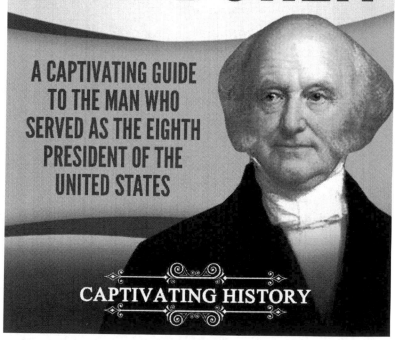

MARTIN
VAN BUREN

A CAPTIVATING GUIDE
TO THE MAN WHO
SERVED AS THE EIGHTH
PRESIDENT OF THE
UNITED STATES

CAPTIVATING HISTORY

A CAPTIVATING GUIDE
TO THE LIFE OF AARON
BURR AND THE MOST
FAMOUS DUEL IN
AMERICAN HISTORY

CAPTIVATING HISTORY

WORLD WAR 2

A CAPTIVATING GUIDE FROM BEGINNING TO END

CAPTIVATING HISTORY

Selected Bibliography

Cohen, Lizbeth. *Making a New Deal: Industrial Workers in Chicago, 1919-1939*. New York: Cambridge University Press, 1990.

Douglas, Ann. *Terrible Honesty: Mongrel Manhattan in the 1920s*. New York: Farrar, Straus and Giroux, 1995.

Gottleib, Peter. *Making Their Own Way: Southern Black Migration to Pittsburgh, 1916-1930*. Urbana IL: University of Illinois Press, 1987.

Lerner, Michael. *Dry Manhattan: Prohibition in New York City*. Cambridge MA: Harvard University Press, 2007.

Osafsky, Gilbert. *Harlem: The Making of a Ghetto*. New York: Harpers and Row, 1963.

Peretti, Burton W. *The Creation of Jazz: Music, Race and Culture in Urban America*. Chicago: University of Illinois Press, 1994.

Pfeffer, Paula. *A. Philip Randolph, Pioneer of the Civil Rights Movement*. Baton Rouge, LA: Louisiana University Press, 1990.

Platt, Harold. *The Electric City: Energy and Growth of the Chicago Area, 1880-1930*. Chicago: University of Chicago Press, 1991.

Spear, Allen. *Black Chicago*. Chicago: University of Chicago Press: 1967.

Susman, Warren I. *Culture as History: The Transformation of American Society in the Twentieth Century*. Washington: Smithsonian Institution Press, 1984.

Wiebe, Robert. *The Search for Order 1877-1920*. New York: Hill and Wang Publishing, 1967.

Free Bonus from Captivating History (Available for a Limited time)

Hi History Lovers!

Now you have a chance to join our exclusive history list so you can get your first history ebook for free as well as discounts and a potential to get more history books for free! Simply visit the link below to join.

Captivatinghistory.com/ebook

Also, make sure to follow us on:

Twitter: @Captivhistory

Facebook: Captivating History:@captivatinghistory

Made in the USA
San Bernardino, CA
14 July 2018